Remembering
Denver

Turner Publishing Company
www.turnerpublishing.com

Remembering Denver

Copyright © 2010 Turner Publishing Company

Library of Congress Control Number: 2010923496

ISBN: 978-1-59652-626-6

Printed in the United States of America

ISBN: 978-1-68336-827-4 (pbk.)